D1250209

THE GILPIN TRAM

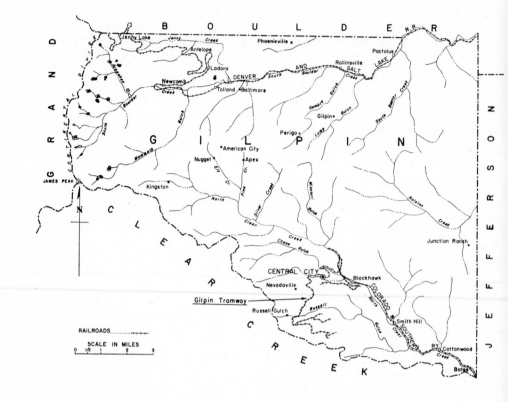

THE GILPIN

TRAM

FRANK R. HOLLENBACK

SAGE BOOKS, *Denver*

Copyright, 1958, by Frank R. Hollenback

Sage Books are published by

Alan Swallow, 2679 So. York, Denver 10, Colo.

Table of Contents

Table of Maps and Illustrations

The Gilpin Tram

A newspaper of 1890 called the Gilpin Tram "a mechanical curiosity" and in the same article referred to it as "a wonderful monument of engineering skill." While it operated under several corporate names during thirty-one years of existence, it was always best known as the Gilpin Tram, or simply as the tram. Its mission was to haul the ore from the mines of Gilpin County, Colorado, to the processing mills and railhead at Black Hawk, and to return with coal and supplies. It negotiated unbelievable curves and grades as it climbed 1600-feet in the course of a few miles.

By providing cheap and efficient transportation, the tram actually upgraded good mineral deposits to profitable orebodies. It was listed in Poor's: a paragraph or two was sufficient to describe its purpose, list the assets, and then the liabilities. The tram's whistle was never heard outside "The Little Kingdom of Gilpin" and was never silent within the realm.

The tram was a mining road first and last. Its life ebbed with the decline of mining in the county. Like many small roads it was first a prized possession and then a liability to a parent railroad. The little two-footer was built by practical men when the need for it became a necessity if mining were to continue prospering in Gilpin County. When the chips were down the tram went in a hurry, probably with less than the small amount of fanfare, if not hostility, which attended its advent.

Historians have not had very much to say about the tram. It

9

was a humble road without glamor. Some of the men who operated the tram are still around to reminisce. Old railroad and county records help fill in the gaps. Practically ignored at first, the little road gained sufficient stature as time went on to merit frequent newspaper paragraphs and articles, each a story in itself.

For proper appreciation of the tram one should walk over the old roadbed. What's left is still "a wonderful monument of engineering skill."

The Background

Exhorbitant ore hauling costs were a serious problem to the mine operators of Gilpin County, Colorado, in the 1880's. Mining was booming but most of the mines were separated by considerable distances and elevations from the ore processing mills. The only method of transporting the ore was by wagon and mule team.

The mills and sampling works were dependent upon large quantities of water and consequently were located at Black Hawk on North Clear Creek. Here was the only adequate and usually dependable source of water in the county. (Not always dependable, either. Water for domestic needs was once distributed and sold in Black Hawk for one dollar a barrel.) A few of the mines had mills adjoining, but from throughout the county most of the ore was brought by wagon and team to Black Hawk for processing. The smelting ore for the furnaces in Denver and Pueblo was also taken to the railhead in Black Hawk, the only rail point in the county. The mines used large quantities of coal. This and other supplies and machinery were hauled to the mines from the railroad by team and wagon.

The narrow-gauge line of the Colorado Central reached Black Hawk in 1872, and Central City over the famous switchback in 1878. This was during a period of great narrow-gauge railroad expansion into the Colorado mining camps following the arrival of the railroad into Denver in 1870.

The railroad naturally benefitted the county, especially the mining industry. But it did not solve the problem of getting the ore from, for example, the 9600-foot high mines of Quartz Hill to the mills in Black Hawk at an altitude of 8000-feet. Not only was this difference in elevation a severe handicap, but also the main

10

Ore wagons in Gregory Gulch. *Western Collection of Denver Public Library.*

and access roads were tortuous and slow, particularly in the winter. The draying charges as a result were exhorbitant. It was an inefficient and expensive method of transporting ore and supplies. On the other hand it was the only method available.

At the same time it is only fair to consider the teamsters' position. Mules were high on the Denver market and mule skinning taxed a man's stamina and morals. But the dray man held high card in the stiff game of mining and set the stakes accordingly. His was the only means of getting the ore from mine to mill, and without a mill a mine is nothing.

In this day and age one can only begin to imagine the time and effort required to get a few tons of ore down by wagon from a mine in Prosser Gulch to a mill in Black Hawk. This was no fair weather business because the ore had to come down day and night, winter and summer. If the roads were blocked by snow the mines were soon without stockpiling space and the mills were forced to shut down. When the ore moved again, there was a double burden on teamsters and mill operators.

The business had other sidelights and problems. There was a story told concerning the high mortality rate of mules one year. It was customary for the teamsters to water their animals at a barrel placed outside the Bobtail Tunnel to catch the mine drainage. After many high-priced mules had expired from, at the moment, unknown causes, it was later discovered that the drainage water contained a high amount of arsenic!

Still, the teamsters were not in want for business. With the mines running at full capacity there was plenty of ore to be hauled. The mills had to be fed and the mines needed coal and supplies.

But what of the mines with low-grade ore so marginal that the high transportation cost prevented their operation? These excessive costs meant the difference between a profitable mine and just a mineral deposit.

The terrain of Gilpin County must be understood in order to appreciate the transportation problem confronting the mine operators in 1885. On the southern end of the county's mineral belt, a 9,600-foot divide separated the watersheds of North and South Clear Creek. Virginia Canon was an obstacle to travel if ore were to be shipped to Idaho Springs. Northerly from the divide the mining area dropped 1600 feet in a distance of only several miles to the mills and railroad on North Clear Creek.

A tramway of sorts had been built in the county fifteen years earlier. Being crude and inefficient, it did not last long. Aerial tramways were out of the question because of only localized and individual benefit. A possible solution to the haulage problem for the upper mines of the county was the Newhouse Tunnel being driven from Idaho Springs toward Quartz Hill. Later a number of mines were connected with the tunnel, but there is no evidence available to indicate that much Gilpin County ore was hauled out of the Newhouse to the South Clear Creek mills.

So there was a very definite need for better transportation to get the complex gold, silver, lead, and copper ores from the outlying mines without mills to the processing plants in Black Hawk. In Gilpin County's system of free enterprise this situation was soon to be remedied.

Corporate Structure

ARTICLES OF INCORPORATION

KNOW ALL MEN BY THESE PRESENTS, that we, Andrew W. Rogers, Henry C. Bolsinger, Bradford H. Locke and Henry J. Hawley

12

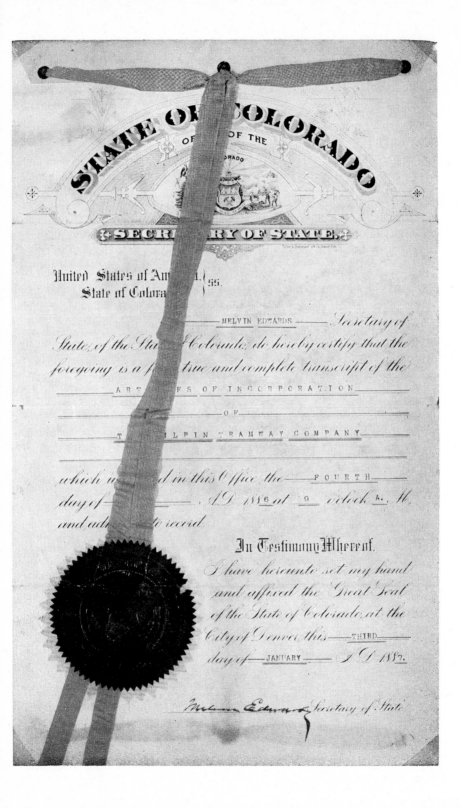

STATE OF COLORADO

OFFICE OF THE

SECRETARY OF STATE.

United States of America, } ss.
State of Colorado

———— MELVIN EDWARDS ———— Secretary of State, of the State of Colorado, do hereby certify that the foregoing is a full, true and complete transcript of the

ARTICLES OF INCORPORATION

OF

THE GILPIN TRAMWAY COMPANY

which was filed in this Office the FOURTH day of ———— A.D. 1886 at 9 o'clock A. M. and admitted to record.

In Testimony Whereof,

I have hereunto set my hand and affixed the Great Seal of the State of Colorado, at the City of Denver, this THIRD day of JANUARY A.D. 1887.

Melvin Edwards Secretary of State.

of Gilpin County and Robert A. Campbell of Arapahoe County, Colorado, do hereby associate ourselves together for the purpose and object of becoming a body corporate under Chapter XIX of the Revised Statutes of the State of Colorado and the several Acts Adamanatory and supplemental thereto, and for that purpose and object do hereby make, execute, acknowledge and deliver these, our Articles of Incorporation.

ARTICLE 1.

The corporate name of this Company shall be THE GILPIN TRAMWAY COMPANY.

ARTICLE 2.

The objects for which the said Company is formed are: (a) To buy, build, operate and sell an iron or steel tramway of two (2) feet gauge, to be operated by steam, horse, compressed air, electric or other suitable power. (b) To acquire by purchase or otherwise the right of way for said tramway together with depot grounds, the necessary buildings and land for ore chutes, bins and platforms.

(c) To transport ore and other materials from the mines to the various mills, sampling works and railroad stations in Central City and Black Hawk.

(d) To transport coal, timbers, lagging and other materials to the several mines or mills, or to some point near the same.

ARTICLE 3.

The capital stock of said Company shall be fifty thousand dollars ($50,000) divided into five thousand shares at ten dollars ($10) cash.

ARTICLE 4.

The time of the commencement of said Company shall be the date of these articles of incorporation and the term of its existence shall be twenty (20) years.

ARTICLE 5.

The number of directors of said Company shall be five and the names of those directors who shall manage the affairs of said Company for the first year of its existence are Andrew W. Rogers, Henry C. Bolsinger, Bradford H. Locke, Robert A. Campbell and Henry J. Hawley.

ARTICLE 6.

The name of the County in which the principal business of said Company shall be carried on is Gilpin County, State of Colorado, and the principal office of said Company shall be kept at Central City in said County and State.

ARTICLE 7.

The stock of said Company shall be non-accessable.

ARTICLE 8.

The board of directors may make such prudential by-laws for the government of said Company as they may see fit.

ARTICLE 9.

The said tramway shall commence at some suitable point near the westerly boundary line of said Gilpin County and run by the most feasible route to Black Hawk with branches leading to Russell Gulch and to the several mines along its main line and to the mills and sampling works and railroad stations in Central City and Black Hawk.

ARTICLE 10.

The management of said Company shall vest in the board of directors, but they may delegate such powers as they see fit to the executive committee consisting of the president, vice president and the secretary and treasurer of the Company each of whom shall be members of said board of directors, which said executive committee shall have full charge of all matters coming under such delegated powers, except when the board of directors shall be in session.

WITNESS our hands and seals this 29th day of July 1886.

Henry C. Bolsinger   (SEAL)
Bradford H. Locke   (SEAL)
Robert A. Campbell   (SEAL)
Andrew W. Rogers   (SEAL)
Henry J. Hawley   (SEAL)

State of Colorado,)
) SS
County of Gilpin,)

I, Edwin E. Chase, a Notary Public within and for said County in the State aforesaid, do hereby certify that Andrew W. Rogers, Henry C. Bolsinger, Bradford H. Locke, Robert A. Campbell, and Henry J. Hawley personally known to me to be the persons whose names are subscribed to the foregoing articles of incorporation, appeared before me this day in person and acknowledged that they signed, sealed and delivered the said instrument of writing as their free and voluntary act for the uses and purposes therein set forth.

Given under my hand and notarial seal this 29th day of July A.D. 1886.

Edwin E. Chase
Notary Public

Notarial Seal

Filed for record this 31st day of July, A.D. 1886 at 2:00 o'clock P.M.

Bart Robbins
County Clerk and Recorder

15

That was it. The complete story of the tramway's origin written in less than 600 words. Almost complete, that is, because soon after construction began it became apparent that capitalization was too low. Ground was broken April 15, 1887, at Black Hawk. Costs were higher than had been anticipated in the original estimate. A need also arose to increase the number of directors from five to seven.

Little or nothing can be learned about the original directors from biographies and history books of Gilpin County. Indirectly it may be surmised that most of the men were connected in one way or another with mining in the county.

A notice appeared in the paper for several weeks prior to February 23, 1888, announcing a stockholder's meeting for that date to consider an increase in the board membership. It was signed by Robert A. Campbell, president, and W. S. Wells, secretary.

The name of Fredrick Kruse, who was to manage the tramway for many years, had not yet appeared on the official company roster. In May of that year another notice was out announcing a stockholder's meeting on June 5, 1888, to consider an increase in capitalization.

Apparently no action had been taken at the February meeting in the matter of increasing the number of directors. However, after the June meeting it was announced that the following members were on the board: Robert A. Campbell, president; B. H. Locke, vice-president; Fredrick Kruse, secretary and treasurer; and W. O. McFarlane, John I. Steen, and W. S. Wells.

The Black Hawk directory of 1888 listed Fredrick Kruse as a grocer and manager of the New York mill. However, a March 11, 1887, item in the Central City paper stated that Fredrick Kruse was closing out his grocery business at Gregory Point in order to devote full time to mining and other interests. Later he was mayor of Central City, a school director, and president of the Rocky Mountain National Bank of that city.

The first published notices of a meeting to amend the articles of incorporation, that is, to increase the capitalization of The Gilpin Tramway Company, appeared April 16, 1888. In the meantime the first trainload of ore over the tramway had come down from the Gunnell on December 14, of the previous year. Now, almost six months later, the management had gained sufficient knowledge

16

Approaching Smith Road above Black Hawk.
Western Collection, Denver Public Library.

Smith Road crossing as it appears today.

17

of the operations and future requirements of the company so that they were able to make a good case for more capital. Many of the stockholders were local residents. It was not difficult to have a quorum at the meeting. The resolution to amend the original certificate and increase the capitalization carried unanimously. Note that some time elapsed before the new certificate was filed and made of record in the county clerk's office.

AMENDMENT

TO

CERTIFICATE OF INCORPORATION

OF

THE GILPIN TRAMWAY COMPANY

We, the undersigned do hereby certify: That every stockholder of The Gilpin Tramway Company was duly notified that a meeting of the stockholders of said Company would be held at the Company's office in Central City, Gilpin County, Colo., on the 5th day of June A.D. 1888, at 12 o'clock M among other things to act upon the proposal of the Board of Directors of said Company to increase the capital stock from fifty thousand dollars ($50,000) to two hundred thousand dollars ($200,000) divided into 20,000 shares at $10 each; and the notice of said meeting was also duly published as required by law.

That upon said 5th day of June 1888 at 12 o'clock M every stockholder of said Company was present either in person or by proxy; every share of stock being duly and legally represented.

That the stockholders meeting was duly organized, and among other business the following was offered:

RESOLVED: That the Capital Stock of this company be increased from $50,000 to $200,000 divided into 20,000 shares of $10 each.

That a vote was taken on said resolution and it was carried unanimously and more than 3/4 of all the stock of said company having voted in favor of such increase as requested by statue it was declared duly carried and so entered in the record book of the Company and the officers of the Company were instructed to file the necessary certificates.

In accordance with said action we make and file this certificate and attach the Corporate Seal of the Company hereto.

	(Signed)	The Gilpin Tramway Company
Fredrick Kruse	by	Robert A. Campbell
Secretary		President

State of Colorado) s
County of Gilpin) s   Robert A. Campbell being duly sworn . . . .
                       that the matter and things stated in said Cer-
                       tificate are true of his own knowledge.
Subscribed and sworn before me
this 21 day August A.D. 1888.

    (Signed)   J. S. Updegraff
                County Clerk

Bradford H. Locke, the tramway engineer and builder, sold his entire holdings in The Gilpin Tramway Company to Idaho Springs parties in February, 1889. This amounted to $26,000 worth of stock for which, the Central City paper speculated, "he got a good round sum." The paper went on to say that "it speaks well for the company to have such capitalists (the Idaho Springs buyers) take hold of an undertaking they see is to prove of immense value to the miners of Gilpin County." Locke, after selling his stock, took an extended trip to Bermuda and England. After returning to Gilpin County he became associated with the Little Josephine Mining Company.

The *Rocky Mountain News* paid tribute to Fredrick Kruse, secretary-treasurer and by then general manager of the tram, when it said on February 10, 1890: "To the latter's shrewd and watchful management the present prosperity and admirable system of the road is largely due. When he took hold of it over a year ago its affairs were in a somewhat crippled condition and the enemies of the enterprise, which were numerous and bitter, were gloating over its approaching dissolution. Careful management has in a few months put it out of danger."

Business was good on the tram in the 1890's, but was it prospering? There would appear to have been no reserves set aside for equipment and improvements. Perhaps the rates were too low or there were too many expensive winter snows to fight.

Whatever the reason, more capital was needed and there was only one way to get it. A meeting of the shareholders was held at the company offices in Central City, April 3, 1899. There were 18,816 out of 20,000 shares represented at the session. The directors were authorized to mortgage The Gilpin Tramway Company for $75,000 by issuing 6% twenty-year bonds. After commenting, the *Denver Republican* had this to say: "The company intends to add another engine and a large number of cars to its rolling stock

19

Tram grade on left,; warming house foundation on right.

in order to attend to its present business as it has more than it can do with the present equipment."

The engine and rolling stock were added but the money didn't come from freight profits. Later the mortgage was to haunt and shadow the road.

The next milestone in the corporate and financial life of The Gilpin Tramway Company was reached in 1906. In 1890 the Colorado Central serving Black Hawk and Central City had been absorbed into the Union Pacific, Denver and Gulf Railroad. In 1899 this same portion became a part of the newly organized Colorado and Southern Railway. It was over this line that the smelting ore from Gilpin County was shipped to Denver after being transferred from the tram at Black Hawk.

In 1904 the Colorado and Southern was scrutinizing The Gilpin Tramway Company. Engineers were sent up to look it over. After receiving favorable reports, the railroad bought controlling stock in the tram. The 20-year tramway charter was to expire two years later on July 26, 1906.

On the 24th day of July, 1906, a certificate of incorporation of

The Gilpin Railroad Company was notarized in Central City by Albert Brooks. The certificate listed O. L. Dines, H. W. Cowan, L. E. Rowland, P. H. Holme, and J. G. McMurray as directors of the new company. Dines was in the firm of Dines, Whitted and Davis, Equitable Building, Denver. Rowland and Holme were in the same office as stenographer and lawyer respectively. Cowan and McMurray were chief engineer and special attorney, respectively, of the Colorado and Southern Railway.

This is what the certificate stated, among other things: To purchase, maintain and operate the railroad and tramway lines formerly owned and operated by The Gilpin Tramway Company. The principal business of the Company shall be carried on in the City and County of Denver and in the counties of Gilpin, Clear Creek, and Boulder. Meeting of the board may be held in the city of New York.

Did this mean that there were plans for expansion into Clear Creek and Boulder counties? If so, they probably were soon dropped.

The Gilpin Tramway Company ceased to exist at midnight, July 29, 1906, by the terms of the charter. The indebtedness of the tramway was taken over by The Gilpin Railroad Company. On August 15, 1906, the Gilpin Railroad Company became the Gilpin Railroad and was so known until the end.

By June 30, 1909, the outstanding funded debt consisted of $67,000 of first mortgage 20-year 6% bonds of the old tramway. The entire capital stock less five shares was pledged to cover the old issue. Two years later the funded debt had climbed to $71,000.

Unfortunately and through no fault of the Colorado and Southern, business fell off from an average of 300 tons per day to about 150 tons per day after the railroad took over the tram. Service was discontinued in January, 1917, and the property was sold a few months later.

Contemporaries — Real and Imaginary

Hall's *History of Colorado,* in describing the Gilpin Tram, has this to say: "It is so radical an improvement over the primitive way for the conveyance of ores, fuel and supplies, it is surprising

21

that the lead taken by the Gilpin Tramway has not been generally followed."

Actually the idea of such a conveyance did not originate with the founders of the tram. It was conceived several years earlier by at least two other organizations which for one reason or another were unable to capitalize on the ideas and principles. There was nothing unique in 1886 in the need for low cost and efficient transportation of ore from mine to mill. Let us say that the founders of the Gilpin Tramway Company were the only ones who successfully built and operated such a system.

The Gilpin County Tram Railway Company was projected in February, 1872, with Edmund Leahy as president and chief engineer. Other officials were Anthony M. D'Arcy, Ben Wisebart, Capt. Oliver M. Ambro, and Col. Sam McNasser. Judge William R. Gorsline was counsel. The First National Bank of Denver and Nathaniel Young Company of Central City were agents. The place of business was listed as Nevadaville. The capital stock was $100,000 in 1000 shares of $100 each.

A newspaper account of February 18, 1872, stated that "application for shares could be made with the company's banker accompanied by a deposit of 10% on each share which will be returned in full without deduction."

The purpose of the line was to transport wood, charcoal, and minerals from the forest of Clear Creek and Gilpin Counties for mining and milling and domestic needs.

The *Denver Tribune* of August 27, 1873, said: "This important enterprise has been spoken of in these columns but we have no idea of length and magnitude of the work of construction. We find in the Black Hawk Journal a complete description of the road and its workings. It was by Edmund Leahy and extended from Peck Gulch and vicinity to Black Hawk and Nevadaville. When completed it will be 30 miles long reaching toward the actual summit of the range. It will not surprise us to see coal and hay coming in from Middle Park by this line within five years. The tram road is a very simple structure.

"The grade has been made the same as the regular grade of the creek. Ties are round timbers, securely bedded, about three feet apart. The rails are pine poles six to eight inches in diameter and about 16-feet long. These are boxed down into the ties with no other fastening required. Curvature of the line is easily provided by proper selection and laying of rails, many having required curvature. Tread of car wheels is broad and flanges deep so that at five or six miles per hour no car has jumped the track. The Nevada branch is as far as Fall River crossing and on the Black Hawk line to Wiley's mill—16 miles of successful operation. There are four or five cars on each branch with two crewmen who also load wood."

That tells just about everything except for the kind of motive power and rolling stock. According to other sources the cars operated by gravity and were returned by horse power.

The *Colorado Miner* of April 18, 1872, quoted the *Black Hawk Journal*: "The tram will put forty men to work in a few days." The enterprise was crude and inefficient. Never profitable, it operated but a short time and was a total financial loss.

The divide separating Central City and Idaho Springs has always been a challenge. Precipitous Virginia Canon and a 9363-foot ridge have hindered travel between the two towns. Were it not for these obstacles, perhaps more ore would have been shipped to the mills in Idaho Springs from Gilpin County. Even to this day people believe there is a connection, however complex, between the Bobtail Tunnel in Black Hawk and the Newhouse or Argo

Old grade on typical rock wall above Chase Gulch.

23

Looking up Chase Gulch in Black Hawk. *Mary Blake.*

Tunnel in Idaho Springs. The latter did extend under Quartz Hill, at least.

An Idaho Springs editor who declaimed at great length about the future of the Gilpin Tram solved the problem of connecting Central City and Idaho Springs by merely tracing a route on a map. However, some heads must have given the matter some real thought. On July 17, 1877, they proposed the Virginia Tram Railroad Company to run to the head of Virginia Canon. What happened to the project?

In 1907, following completion of the Denver, Northwestern and Pacific Railroad up South Boulder Canon, the Pactolus Road was projected. The correct name for the proposed line was the Gilpin and Clear Creek District Railway. Elaborate promotional brochures stated that the route would begin at Pactolus on the Moffat Road and proceed up Beaver Creek, thence over Dory Hill, crossing the lower end of Missouri Gulch to the north fork of Clear Creek. From there it would cross the head of Chase Gulch and continue on to Central City, a total of 19½ miles. Terminal lines were to be extended to Black Hawk, Nevadaville, and Russell Gulch, an additional eight miles. It was to be standard gauge.

The brochures were well done. The text stressed the need for standard-gauge passenger and freight service into the region, talked about the scenic views along the way (showing Moffat Road pictures of the high country) and sneered at the existing narrow-gauge service. It proposed through traffic from Denver to Central City to be handled by two passenger trains a day in both directions. Remains of the old grade can be seen today along Beaver Creek.

But getting back into the realm of two-foot tramways: "The lead taken by the Gilpin Tramway" did not go completely unnoticed. In March, 1889, Col. E. E. Pray came over from Aspen to study the Gilpin Tram. He was one of a party interested in building a similar line from Aspen to the Pitkin County mines. On March 20, 1889, it was announced that a company with a capital stock of $100,000 had been organized in Aspen for the purpose of transporting ore from the mines to the smelters and railroads. On April 4, 1889, work was to begin as soon as frost left the ground. What happened to this project?

Eight years after they founded the Gilpin Tram a bold, new railroad venture was proposed by a group of tram officials.

On August 8, 1894, Fredrick Kruse, Robert A. Campbell, Thomas H. Porter, Joseph Bostwick, and William A. Wells appeared before H. A. Hicks, county judge, Gilpin County, with a Certificate of Incorporation of the Gilpin James Peak & Middle Park Railway. The capitalization was from $100,000 with 1000

This was the box culvert bridge in Russell Gulch.

25

Tucker mine branch off main line at head of Chase Gulch.
Western Collection, Denver Public Library.

accessable shares at $100 each. The life of the railway was to be 50 years dating from September 1, 1894.

This was a truly ambitious project. Study of the proposed route explains the need for an accessable stock set-up: "Beginning in the city of Black Hawk, county of Gilpin, thence up North Clear Creek and along the line, track and grading of the old Gilpin Tram Railway Company to a point at or near Mammoth Gulch and Elk Park . . . thence by the most practicable route down and along the Frazer River to the Grand River; thence down and along the Grand River to Hot Sulphur Springs; and also a line from some point below said canon on said Frazer River by the most practicable route to and in the direction of Grand Lake on the Grand River to Grand Lake. Said line or railroad to run through the Counties of Gilpin, Clear Creek and Grand in the State of Colorado."

The instrument did not specify the gauge of the proposed line (presumably two-feet), nor did it designate any industry or field to be served. The idea was possibly an elaboration of the old tram railway scheme, salvaging some of the latter's physical features for use of the proposed new line. (Note a reference to the old track.)

Here was another early Colorado paper railroad which probably didn't even attain blueprint status.

Track, Engines, and Rolling Stock

Thirty-five pound iron and steel rail was used on the two-foot gauge track specified in the Articles of Incorporation. By April 15, 1887, Tierney and Harrington, the contractors, had graded

Some places they struck rock! *Western Collection, Denver Public Library.*

one-third miles on the hillside above Chase Gulch with a force of 30 men. The grade was several hundred feet up on the hill. This height was necessary in order to gain elevation into Central City and was attained by starting the switchback from Clear Creek about three-quarter miles above Black Hawk.

Grading this section was not difficult except for several rock cuts. Rather than making side-hill cuts the grade on the hillside was usually carried by rock walls filled with earth and stone. Rock walls without mortar were common in the area at that time. Today these walls and the grade can be seen above highway 119 and the road up Chase Gulch. J. H. Tierney, one of the contractors, was skilled in this type of construction.

Actual track-laying was begun June 29, 1887, near the depot in "upper" Black Hawk. Whether it was done by the contractors or by crews of the tramway company is not known. By July 27 two miles of track had been laid and it was expected that the rails would reach Eureka Street in Central City the following week. If the chronological record is correct, all of first track laying was done without the use of a work train. The first engine was not delivered in Black Hawk until August 24.

Bradford H. Locke was in charge of engineering and construction. Samuel A. Rank assisted in the surveying. The road was built as cheaply as possible with a minimum of cuts and fills. Rights-of-way were no problem. In fact, there were no formal agreements except with the railroad on whose narrow-gauge track

The capition says: Tramway depot, Black Hawk, Colorado.
Western Collection, Denver Public Library.

28

Grade above Chase Gulch.

a third rail was laid for the tram in the vicinity of Black Hawk. There were two other exceptions where the line was privately owned and these are noted on the map. A mine desiring a connection with the tram would make a deposit to show good faith and thus prevent the tram from sponsoring promotional schemes at its own expense.

By September 28 the line reached the Gunnell dump, having completed the switchback in Nevadaville. It was progressing toward the Prize and Hubert mines.

The many bridges along the way were little more than rock filling built around box culverts. There were fifty-foot radius curves and grades exceeding four per cent, sometimes reaching five or more.

Meanwhile a Shay locomotive and dump cars had been ordered. The Shay was the ideal engine for the tramway operations. It had been invented by a lumberman, E. E. Shay of Bar Harbor, Michigan, a few years before and in 1879 the locomotive was being manufactured and sold by the Lima Machine Works in Lima, Ohio. It had cylinders on one side from which power was transmitted through a line shaft to pinions geared to the drivers. The shaft lengthened and shortened according to the curvature of the track.

29

Typical rock fill and box culvert in gully.

The tender, instead of being dead weight, was an integral part of the engine. When tramway officials placed the order there were many Shays in use around the country on mining and lumber roads.

The first Shay locomotive with builder's number 181 arrived in Black Hawk August 10, 1887. A news item in the local paper said that it attracted considerable attention, "from young and old alike." It had two 7 x 7 cylinders, a cap stack, 24-inch drivers, and weighed ten tons without water or coal. It was given road No. 1 and named the Gilpin.

It was not until September 21 that the first fourteen cars arrived. These were of one-half cord capacity, four wheel truck, with bottom dump hoppers.

At this point there are some contradictions in the accounts of the tram's progress. One account stated, on September 21, that the track had been completed beyond the shafthouse on Winnebago Hill. Another story on July 27 said the track was to reach Central City the following week. There may have been some delay.

The tram was soon in business after the arrival of engine and cars. A newspaper story on October 5 said that one Henry Becker was mourning the loss of a dog killed by the tramway engine. The first train on the tramway brought down six one-half cord cars and delivered them to the Meade mill in Black Hawk December 14, 1887.

Accidents more serious than killing a dog began to occur on the tramway, the first in a long series of mishaps. The Central City paper reported on December 28 that "the locomotive Gilpin jumped the track in Central and landed bottomsides-up in the backyard of a Mr. Mitchell. Engineer Stark was held responsible

Water stop at Eureka Street, Central City. *Louis Pircher.*

31

because of running too fast. A force of men from the Eureka Foundry placed the machine on the track and after being overhauled was doing business again."

In January, 1888, more iron rail was en route to extend the tram an additional five miles from the terminal in Nevadaville to the principal mines of Russell Gulch. It was hoped that the second locomotive would be received about February 1. Bradford Locke was at Lima and wrote that the locomotive should arrive about March 1. Locke had just signed a contract for $15,000 worth of new cars. Back in Gilpin County the extension into Russell was progressing and the new engine was shipped from Lima and was to be named Russell. Bridges were being strengthened and the roadbed generally improved.

When the Russell was delivered in Black Hawk the builder's No. 199 was changed to road No. 2. It was slightly larger than No. 1 and weighed 12 tons. Also double trucked, it had three 7 x 7 cylinders, 24-inch drivers, and a cap stack.

Business was good on the tram. By May 8, 1889, the company owned twenty ¾ cord cars, fifty one-cord cars, ten flats, and two locomotives. Two trains a day hauled 71,986 tons of ore in 1889. In the same year 3600 tons of coal and wood were hauled up to the mines.

In May, 1889, the main and branch lines added up to 11 miles. Twenty new one-cord cars and two locomotives were on order at Lima. Fredrick Kruse went back to inspect the cars and make further arrangements for the locomotives. Later in the month the newspaper reported that Kruse and James Thompson, the superintendent, went over the entire line and laid out jobs for the section gang.

Road engine No. 3 left Lima in January, 1890, with builder's No. 264. This one had a diamond stack, weighed 31,000 pounds, and had three 8 x 8 cylinders.

Up to 1890 the total outlay had been $225,000 of which $165,000 was spent on construction. By now the company owned 90 one-cord steel cars. The ten flats had been converted to coal cars with removable sides. Business was good in the 90's but returns apparently were not good enough. The company sold bonds to raise $75,000 for new equipment and improvements.

Road engine No. 4 was shipped from Ohio in February, 1900. Its builder's No. 594 indicates that by then many Shays were in

Heading for the mill at Black Hawk. Note wireless tower. *William Ziege.*

operation. No. 4 had a straight stack and weighed 34,800 pounds, more than three times the weight of engine No. 1. It also had three 8 x 8 cylinders and 24-inch drivers.

Engine No. 5, builder's No. 696, followed almost two years later. Shipped March, 1902, it had the same specifications as No. 4 except that it weighed 36,200 pounds.

When the Colorado and Southern Railway bought control of The Gilpin Tramway Company on February 24, 1904, the motive power and rolling stock consisted of the following:

    3   engines
137   one-cord cars (one cord equals app. eight tons)
    4   ten-ton coal cars
    8   six-ton coal cars
    1   observation car (21 passenger)
    1   water car

Three new pieces of equipment were added immediately:

    1   caboose
    1   four wheel snow plow
    1   rail car

Being too light for the work, engines Nos. 1 and 2 had been sold to mining interests in New Mexico for use on the Silver City, Pinos Altos and Mongollon line.

Spurs and sidings had been built all the way along in addition to

GILPIN TRAMWAY CO.
ENGINES 3-4-5
SHAY GEARED
BUILT BY LIMA LOCO. & MACH. CO.

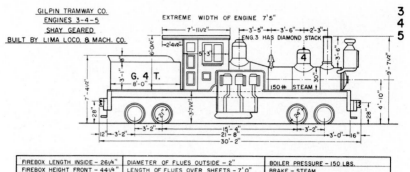

FIREBOX LENGTH INSIDE – 26¼"	DIAMETER OF FLUES OUTSIDE – 2"	BOILER PRESSURE – 150 LBS.
FIREBOX HEIGHT FRONT – 44¼"	LENGTH OF FLUES OVER SHEETS – 7'0"	BRAKE – STEAM
FIREBOX HEIGHT REAR – 44¼"	HEATING SURFACE FIREBOX – 47.55 SQ. FT.	3 CYL. 8" DIA. X 8" STROKE
FIREBOX WIDTH TOP – 30"	HEATING SURFACE FLUES – 175.68 SQ. FT.	TENDER CAPACITY WATER – 900 GAL.
FIREBOX WIDTH BOTTOM – 30"	HEATING SURFACE TOTAL – 223.23 SQ. FT.	TENDER CAPACITY COAL – 2 TONS
NUMBER OF FLUES – 48"	GRATE AREA – 5.47 SQ. FT.	TOTAL WEIGHT –

GILPIN TRAMWAY CO.
RAIL CAR
NO. 01

01

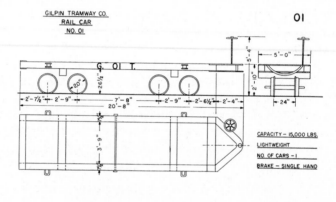

CAPACITY – 15,000 LBS.
LIGHTWEIGHT
NO. OF CARS – 1
BRAKE – SINGLE HAND

GILPIN TRAMWAY CO.
SNOW PLOW
NO. 02

02

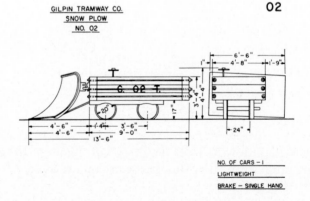

NO. OF CARS – 1
LIGHTWEIGHT
BRAKE – SINGLE HAND

GILPIN TRAMWAY CO.
FLAT CAR
NO. 1-2-3

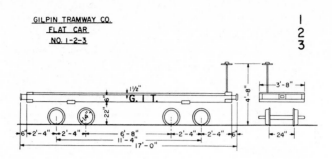

"G. I. T."

CAPACITY — 8,000 LBS.

LIGHTWEIGHT

NO. OF CARS — 3

BRAKE — SINGLE HAND

GILPIN TRAMWAY CO.
FLAT CAR
NO. 4

4

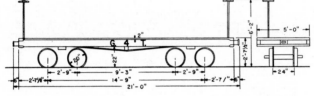

"G 4 T."

CAPACITY — 20,000 LBS.

LIGHTWEIGHT

NO. OF CARS — 1

BRAKE — DOUBLE HAND

GILPIN TRAMWAY CO.
COAL CAR
NO. 5

5

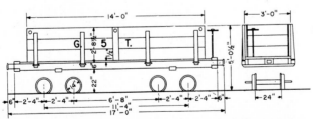

G. 5 T.

CAPACITY — 8,000 LBS.

LIGHTWEIGHT

NO. OF CARS — 1

BRAKE — SINGLE HAND

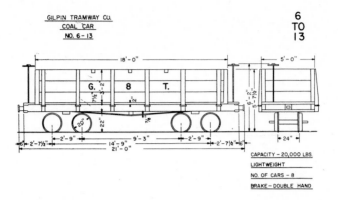

GILPIN TRAMWAY CO.
COAL CAR
NO. 6 - 13

6
TO
13

G. 8 T.

CAPACITY – 20,000 LBS.
LIGHTWEIGHT
NO. OF CARS – 8
BRAKE – DOUBLE HAND

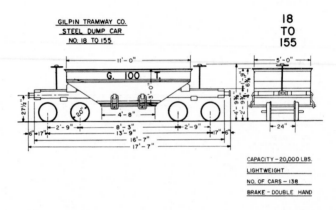

GILPIN TRAMWAY CO.
STEEL DUMP CAR
NO. 18 TO 155

18
TO
155

G. 100 T.

CAPACITY – 20,000 LBS.
LIGHTWEIGHT
NO. OF CARS – 138
BRAKE – DOUBLE HAND

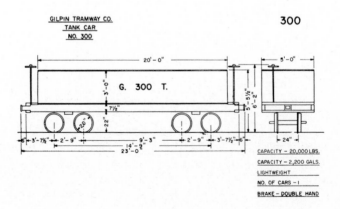

GILPIN TRAMWAY CO.
TANK CAR
NO. 300

300

G. 300 T.

CAPACITY – 20,000 LBS.
CAPACITY – 2,200 GALS.
LIGHTWEIGHT
NO. OF CARS – 1
BRAKE – DOUBLE HAND

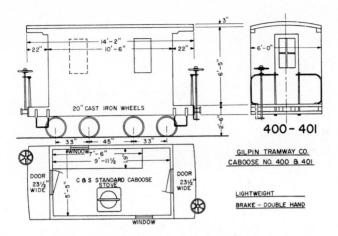

400 - 401

GILPIN TRAMWAY CO.
CABOOSE NO. 400 & 401

LIGHTWEIGHT
BRAKE - DOUBLE HAND

numerous branch lines. The four-switchback Banta Hill line was built around 1907. This 3.78-mile extension was the last of any size and the first to be taken out because of the light traffic over it. Constructed by a crew of approximately thirty Japanese, the line was paid for by the mining company at Banta Hill.

In August and September of 1904 the entire line was chained by D. S. Hooker and party. From the survey data a map, at least semi-official, was made. This qualifying statement is used because the title block, legend, and track identification used incorrectly the name Gilpin County Tramway. If the name The Gilpin Tramway Company, as it appears in the articles of incorporation, is proper then all other forms and titles are in error. Perhaps the Gilpin County Tramway name was used so often it became fixed in the memories of those who were familiar with The Gilpin Tramway Company's predecessor.

At this point it may be well to review the names under which the tramway operated. From July, 1886, until July, 1906, it was The Gilpin Tramway Company. When the Colorado and Southern took over it became The Gilpin Railroad Company for several months and then simply as the Gilpin Railroad until the end.

The map was published on July 1, 1905. Some liberties have been taken in reproducing it: certain features were deleted and others added. The following tram mileages are shown:

37

Doubleheader up with coal, Quartz Hill.
Western Collection, Denver Public Library.

Main line from Colorado and Southern transfer at Black Hawk
to—

End of track at Frontenac mine	7.92 miles
End of track at Banta Hill	11.70 miles
Fullerton mill branch	0.81 miles
Concrete branch switchback	0.94 miles
Pease Kansas branch	0.68 miles
Phoenix Burroughs branch	1.07 miles
Quartz Hill switchback	2.09 miles
Saratoga branch	1.28 miles
Total main line and branches (less Banta Hill)	14.79 miles
Total miles of sidings and spurs	5.52 miles
Spurs branching from C.& S. Ry.	1.04 miles
Grand Total July 1, 1905	21.35 miles

The Banta Hill extension is shown on the map but not included
in the mileage totals. If it were, the grand total would become
26.13 miles.

Frontenac mine at original end of track. Note branch grade below.

R. C. Martin owned 0.51 miles of sidings and spurs not included in the total. Also not included was the Tucker mine branch.

Note that all Mile Posts are based on Colorado and Southern Railway distances from Denver. The tramway had trackage rights on the Colorado and Southern from the end of Colorado and Southern track to a point east of Black Hawk for which the tram paid a yearly rental of $1000.

The picture of the Democratic convention delegates entraining for a trip over the tram on July 11, 1908, merits study. It was taken by the mother of Charles and James Robbins of Black Hawk and processed by her in the days when home darkrooms were not common. The picture was taken alongside the Polar Star mill. This was the place tram excursionists were transferred from the Colorado and Southern trains. It was also the spot where smelting ore was dumped from the tram hoppers to the narrow-gauge cars. Note the reflection and shine on the metal plate in the chute where ore passed over it. The ore cars bore the lettering GRR whereas the coal cars fitted for passengers were still lettered G.T.—almost two years after the line changed hands.

39

Lou Pircher tells about the trouble one summer with caterpillars. Hoards of caterpillars on the track out of Prosser Gulch made it difficult or impossible for engines to get traction on the steep hill. Sand was of little help. Finally Lou installed metal brushes on the locomotives and swept away the pests.

The original light iron was replaced in 1910 with 40-pound Colorado and Southern steel rail on the entire line.

After this there was no need for more engines and cars. Mining began to decline and with it ore traffic on the tram. According to Lou Pircher, superintendent from 1904 to 1913, the engines didn't require much attention or maintenance. Probably the cars didn't either. In any event it was a case of make-do.

Otto Blake recalls that the track didn't get much attention toward the end, either. Otto was the salvage foreman. He says the spikes and rail came up without much trouble when his crew pulled up the track.

The first load of ore over the tramway . . . .

It is generally conceded that construction on the tram was started in the fall of 1886, following formation of the company the previous summer. It probably was, but the record shows that only one-third miles had been graded by April 15, 1887.

The tram enterprise didn't get off to a very good start with the residents of the county. Many people had connections directly or indirectly with the ore-hauling business and resented the probable inroads the tram would make.

A reporter, writing in the *Rocky Mountain News* of February 10, 1890, and reviewing the progress of the tram, put it this way: "The construction of this wonderful monument of engineering skill was commenced in the fall of 1886. Like all enterprises of a daring nature, it met with the most senseless and invidious opposition from the very businessmen whose prosperity depended upon its completion. It was laughed at and derided as the product of a dazed brain, but the engineer for the company, Bradford H. Locke, pushed it through to the mines of Russell Gulch. The teamsters, seeing their occupation gone, treated the invasion with the same selfish and obdurant folly with which the hackman regards the cable car."

The article went on to say that the charges for ore hauling made

40

The snowplow got this far anyway in the big 1913 snow. *William Ziege.*

by the teamsters were so extortionate as to drive many a good mine out of business. The tramway immediately reduced ore hauling charges by at least one-half. The rates charged by the new carrier were about $.75 per ton but varied according to the distance of the mine from mill.

The 1888 directory of Black Hawk listed 13 mills (and 14 saloons) in the town—all presumably in operation. The mills were:

> Arrighi & White
> Becker
> Cashier
> Empire
> Gregory-Bobtail
> Hidden Treasure
> Humphry concentrator
> Fullerton, upper
> Meade
> New York
> Polar Star
> Randolph
> Wheeler & Sullivan

By May 29, 1889, a total of 20 stamp mills were in operation. Not all, of course, were served by the tram.

The first load of ore over the tramway was hauled on December 14, 1887, from the Grand Army shaft at the Gunnell to the Meade mill of William Fullerton.

The advent of the tram did or did not increase the mineral production in Gilpin County depending upon which set of figures is used. The *Rocky Mountain News* of February 10, 1890, published this data for the county:

1885	$2,374,175
1886	2,718,380
1887	2,479,187
1888	2,695,157
1889	3,334,300

Clearing the line to the Gunnell. Note lettering. *William Ziege.*

These figures would indicate that the tram had a definite part in the increased production.

On the other hand Henderson's *Mining in Colorado* gives this information:

1885	$2,409,408
1886	1,480,327
1887	1,488,519
1888	1,538,566
1889	1,437,182

This shows an anomaly which is hard to reconcile.

A Gilpin County mine operator being interviewed by a *News* reporter on April 17, 1889, had this to say: "Yes, we are taking out a greater quantity of ore this season, more perhaps than ever before at so early a date in the year."

The reporter then mentioned that he had not seen many ore wagons on this trip compared with previous visits in the area.

To this the mining man replied, "One cause for that is the same that increases the output. You know we built a tramway last year. That tramway, a two-foot railway, climbs over the mountains with

Pause at Eureka Street, Central City. Note snowplow. *William Ziege.*

43

the ease of a burro, only with much greater speed, and now it is connected on the main line by spurs with two-thirds of the great mines in the camp, affording direct rail connection with the mills at Black Hawk and the Colorado Central depot at fully 25% less cost than could be done with wagons. This reduction in freight enables the mines to ship a lower grade of ore at a profit. Hence, ores are now sent to the mills and smelters that could not heretofore be mined at a profit."

These statements seem to summarize pretty well the objectives of the tram's founders. Despite one set of figures to the contrary, it would seem to be only logical that the tram would certainly increase the production and value of ore in the county.

But if it were thought that the tram would be an all-weather line, there was another thought coming. Winter struck hard in February, 1899. The *News* of February 5 said, "Owing to the severe storm of last week and the inability of the Gilpin Tram to get through snow drifts to haul the ore out, the Kansas-Burroughs properties are temporarily closed down as every ore bin is filled and every possible place to store the ore is piled full. In a few days the accumulation of ore will have to be moved and the mines will

Snow troubles. Was one stalled? *William Ziege.*

44

All manpower and equipment fought the big snow in 1913. *William Ziege.*

resume again. A number of other mines are closed on the same account. The storm may be the cause of decreased output from the Gilpin mines this month."

Old timers said the storm was the worst they could remember. Three weeks elapsed after the last shipment left the Topeka because of the blockade on the tram. Two loads of ore were sent to Idaho Springs for milling, two days were required to make the trip.

The *News* headlined on March 6, 1899:

Badly Hindered In Gilpin County

The Severest Winter in Recollection of Oldest Settler

Gilpin Tram Blocked in Reaching the Chief Ore Producers

Material Blocked Out In the Stopes

Engine No. 3 overturned at Prosser Gulch Dec. 29, 1897.
Western Collection, Denver Public Library.

Miners Laid Off Until Mills and Smelters
Can Be Reached — Summer Shipment Will Be Heavy

Despite the storm and blockade, the Kansas-Burroughs shipped
429 tram cars of ore, or 2178 tons, from March 7 to March 28,
1899.

From all the foregoing it is apparent that the mining industry
was fully dependent upon the tram. By the same token it was
taken for granted as a permanent fixture in the county. Now
the press was friendly, regularly printing news about the line and
the people who operated it.

The tram was a natural for accidents. No air brakes and no rules
of the road. For instance, engine No. 3, going up the hill on December 29, 1897, with a long string of loaded cars, jumped the
track on the bridge over Prosser Gulch. It plunged into the gulch
pinning Harry W. Pierce, the engineer. His body "which had been
cooked by steam," was extricated several hours later. Will Frank-
lin, the fireman, was badly scalded and incurred severe hip in-
juries. The accident was probably caused by tight universals on
the engine.

There were bright sides, too, and business was good. In February, 1898, there had been a slight falling off of smelter ore shipments. Two of the engines were out of commission for the better part of a month. Ore could not be moved. A writer of the day said that "with the arrival of the two machines the line will be in shape to handle all of the ore offered and the mine owners will add to their force and work their properties on a larger scale than ever before."

The February, 1898, output of the Concrete mine in Prosser Gulch was 1500 tons of mill ore. The manager, a Mr. Newell, said that if the tramway would furnish enough cars the monthly output could be 2250 tons of ore.

Every morning the up train or trains would bring the coal and empty ore cars for distribution to the mines. Occasionally there would be machinery and supplies. Empties ordered the previous day were switched to the mine spurs. Then began the job of collecting the loaded cars. The tram engines and rolling stock were equipped only with link and pin couplers, and hand brakes at the ends of the cars. Two experienced brakemen could handle a train on the down grade, using brake clubs and assistance from the steam brake on the engine.

Occasionally trainmen would ride the cars down the hill. Not many cars, just a few at one time. One February night fireman Jimmy Tabb rode a car of concentrates down from the Avon mill in Nevadaville. It was late and for some reason the car had not been coupled to the train. Tabb lost control while trying to keep ahead. The car derailed at Roundhouse Curve, plunged into Clear Creek, and crushed the fireman.

Tough grades show up in short distances. *Francis Rizzari Collection.*

Tram didn't put this teamster out of business. Note third rail.
Francis Rizzari Collection.

Upon arrival in Black Hawk ore cars were switched to the various mills. Each had facilities for dumping the ore into bins. Smelting ore destined for the valley was dumped from a ramp near the Polar Star mill directly into Colorado and Southern cars. This ramp is shown in the convention picture.

In the winter the mill ore was usually frozen in the hoppers, having been very wet in the mine. Then the cars were switched to the warming house which was an ingenious device for thawing the ore. It was a stone building 245-feet long, 28-feet wide, and seven feet high. Three tracks ran the entire length with a drop of nine feet. Heat was provided by steam pipes between the track and three warming stoves. Sometimes the temperature in the building reached 120 degrees but even this heat was not always sufficient to loosen the frozen ore. Charles Robbins recalls seeing men beating and pounding the ore for hours to loosen it for free flow into the ore bins. If thawed or loosened, the ore was delivered to the mill the next morning.

Louis Pircher was with the tramway fifteen years. He started with the company in 1898 and became superintendent in 1904, succeeding Andy Flickenstine. Lou left the tram in 1913 to become boiler inspector for the Moffat Road at Tabernash. Following this he was with the Union Pacific in Denver and retired on March 13, 1948—fifty years to the day in railroading.

Lou lived in the "lace house" in Black Hawk while he was with the tram. He recalls being unable to sleep at night until he heard the tram whistle at the Freedom. This was a signal that everything was all right. He tells about the time fifteen loaded cars got away at the Dogtown Wye and piled up on top of each other, spilling ore all over the track. Before the accident, the ore was just run-of-mine rock. When the claims began to come it was found that the ore had suddenly become very valuable! Years later when Lou and Charlie Niccum, who had been conductor at the time, got together they agreed that kids must have released the brakes.

Cars loaded with frozen ore were too rigid and would not stay on the track. Pircher remembers one time when a frozen car toppled into a mill pond where it had to be cut up with a torch. The ore was literally carried back up by the bucketful.

Excessive speed rarely caused accidents. Top speed for a Shay was about 20 miles per hour. The engine was designed for the long, hard pull, and not for speed. Trains going up traveled about seven miles per hour; the loads down did not exceed eight.

The big snow of 1913 tied up the tram for days. The first day was spent shoveling and clearing the track from Black Hawk to the roundhouse. After that it was fight all the way up the hill. Finally a train with badly needed coal reached Dogtown. (Dogtown was just below Russell.) As it was too late to deliver the coal

Snow at Topeka mine, 1913. *Western Collection, Denver Public Library.*

49

that night, the train was left standing. The next morning not a piece of coal was left.

Charley Robbins remembers the tram with the impressions of a small boy. He lived across the road from the Polar Star mill where excursionists changed trains from Colorado and Southern to tram and back. It was also the place where smelting ore was transferred from tram to the narrow-gauge cars. Charley recalls what he did the day the Democrats came up from the convention to ride on the tram. He says he just stood in one spot and stared. His mother took pictures and processed them at home.

Robbins can still hear the two toots given by the engineer when he called for brakes. Or the three toots which sent the brakemen scrambling over the cars to release the brakes. He remembers how the employees used to beat the frozen ore for hours at a time and how the coal was shoveled laboriously from the Colorado and Southern to the tram cars. Yes, Charley remembers the old days. Today he can tell a story about every foot of track if you can get him to walk along the grade with you. Along with several generations of Gilpin kids, he hitched rides from one end of the line to the other and lived to tell about it.

George William fired tramway engines in 1909 and 1910, usually for Ernie Klein, who died in 1956. George is the brother of the one-time sheriff, Oscar Williams, and spends the summers in Ward. After leaving the tram he went to firing Colorado and Southern engines between Denver and Pueblo. He tells that after firing the small tram engines, he couldn't take it on the big locomotives. It only took two or three tons of coal to get up into Russell Gulch.

Williams hasn't forgotten the day he went up with two cars of lumber behind the engine. At Smith Curve the two cars toppled the engine. George jumped clear of the engine and a broken steam line. He ran back two cars before he remembered Klein in the locomotive. He hurried back and found Klein unscratched. There were no cranes to put engines and cars back on the track—just frogs, jacks, and manpower.

It was common practice for employees coming off shift to ride empties consigned to the mill below Black Hawk. Not all hand brakes worked and it was often necessary to scratch around to find a brake that would stop the car. One night Williams' brother-in-law, Ray Thompson, was hit by a brake chain. It broke an arm and leg. All those present were required to write a report about the accident. Williams says he almost got fired for what he wrote.

Another former tram employee who is around to tell about it is Peter Lind, a Boulder resident. He worked as fireman, brakeman, and conductor from 1905 to 1907. After leaving Gilpin County he went to Como and fired Colorado and Southern engines running to Leadville and Gunnison.

Lind recalls vividly the time he was coupling a lumber car. The engineer acknowledged the back-up signal but the next one was obscured by escaping steam. While making the connection Lind's mitten became frozen on the coupling metal. He was pinned at the hips between the two cars and dragged several feet. Then he was paralyzed from the hips down. The engineer reported the accident by phone from the nearest mine. Lou Pircher at the other

Engine No. 4 in for repairs. *Louis Pircher.*

51

end ordered full speed in bringing the injured man to Black Hawk. It was a fast ride. When the train reached Black Hawk, Dr. J. A. Richmond was waiting and began treatment immediately. Lind was walking again in a few days.

Lind recalls that it was often nip and tuck to have enough engine boiler water on hand to get from here to there and back again. Once it was necessary to borrow water from a mine which was a water customer of the tramway's. Due to acid in the mine water, some of the mines could not use this water for the boilers. The tram had a water car which was used to distribute water to these mines.

The first load of ore over the tramway was hauled December 14, 1887. No one noticed or recorded the exact time the last load of ore was hauled.

Excursions, Tours, and Picnics

The tramway management was not blind to tourist possibilities as another source of revenue for the line. If ore hauling ranked first, coal and supply business second, then development of the tourist market was considered as the third source of income. The first two were soon proved; the latter was unknown.

Certainly the setting was right. The tram followed a scenic course as it climbed a thousand feet in a few miles from Black Hawk to Quartz Hill. Hardly sensational, but good. Mines and mills along the route made a good attraction for any tourist, let alone "gold-minded" ones.

The Gulf Road was running numerous excursions over the line into Black Hawk. What then could be more logical than a passenger interchange somewhere along the common track shared in town by the tram and the railroad, and a trip for the last leg over the Gilpin Tram?

It wasn't until after the tram was opened for freight traffic that an announcement was made for the first excursion over the line. The Central City paper of May 26, 1888, stated "that shortly dodgers will be issued announcing excursions to Black Hawk where connections will be made with the Gilpin Tramway, transfer of passengers made, and from there on . . . over the line of the

First tramway excursion, 1888. *Western Collection, Denver Public Library.*

Tramway to Quartz Hill." At that point the writer was carried away. He concluded that "the scenery over the latter line cannot be excelled as there is one continual change. These excursions will become decidedly popular with tourists and others."

The first tramway excursion was made on June 7, 1888. The special train from Denver stopped at the Polar Star mill in Black Hawk. The tram locomotive Russell coupled to four excursion and one flat car was waiting. Passengers were transferred and the train set out for Quartz Hill. On arrival it was switched to the California mine spur where the excursionists "took in the plant of machinery and surroundings at the mine." On the return the train stopped at the Quartz Hill depot where "a spread, brought from Nelson's in Denver, was served." Again the reporter was voluble. He wrote, "This enterprise in the near future will become the most scenic line of rail travel in Northern Colorado, if not in the state. The first trip over this great scenic line was a decided success, and greatly enjoyed by the excursionists."

Study of the picture which was captioned "Picnic on the Gilpin Tramway, June 7, 1888," shows no evidence of the "spread." This may have been the counterpart of today's camera stops on railroad club excursions.

Even before this first excursion the editor of the *Idaho Springs Gazette* was, to put it mildly, enthusiastic about the tram's future as a scenic line. Here is what he wrote in May, 1888:

CLEAR CREEK AND GILPIN COUNTIES CONNECTED

The Gilpin County Tramway, which at first was not considered feasible, now promises to be one of the wonders of the 19th century. Like Tennyson's brook it "winds about and in and out," taking in all mines and veins. At present it is used principally in transporting ores to the Black Hawk mills, but we understand the C.C. company has joined hands with the tram promoters, and that the road will be extended indefinitely. Observation cars have been constructed and in the near future the tourist will be able to view the famous gold fields of Gilpin from the heights of Bellview Mountain. From thence the train glides down Virginia Canon, and over the hills adjacent, taking in the prominent mines of the region, the Mascot and others.

Here it crosses the canon in a westerly direction and takes a direct shoot for Freeland and Ute Creeks, following the side of the mountain until it reaches Lake Edith. Then turning to the left, a few miles brings it to the famous Chicago Lakes, the highest bodies of fresh water in the Rockies.

Now we are ready to start the return via Echo Lake, Chicago Creek, Idaho Springs and Forks Creek and back to Black Hawk, making one grand complete circle. When completed it will be the main attraction of the American continent!

If the editor had his way it surely would have been the main attraction on the American continent.

The excursion idea on the tram apparently took hold. Other trips were made in 1888. There is nothing to show whether the excursions were profitable for the company.

In June of the following year the tram employees decided to hold a picnic in Russell Park on the Fourth of July—traveling there by tram, of course. Handbills were distributed announcing the event and the train schedules so that residents of Black Hawk, Central City, and Nevadaville could make plans to take a trip over the line at the same time. The five car train reached the park without mishap. It returned immediately to Black Hawk to pick up a baseball club from Golden who were to play the Black Hawk Boosters at the park. The game was delayed because one car jumped the track five times. The game eventually was played but

Democrats on excursion July 11, 1908. Note car lettering.
James and Charles Robbins.

the visitors from Golden lost. They were tired out from the exertion of getting the tram car back on the track so many times.

Another excursion over the tram took place on July 30 of the same year. Senator Henry M. Teller and other notables were aboard as guests of the tram officials. A reporter who rode the train noted that many improvements had been made since his last trip over the road.

The Democratic National Convention was held in Denver in July, 1908. As a part of the windup some 650 people who attended the convention left the Denver Union Station in two special trains on the morning of July 11 and arrived in Black Hawk two hours later. Little did they realize what was in store for them. They toured the Fifty Gold Mines mill and then got aboard two tramway specials. One observer says today that the confusion was unbelievable. Another equally reliable witness tells that the transfer was made in an orderly manner without delay. Coal cars and other pieces of rolling stock had been draped with red, white, and blue bunting and equipped with benches for the passengers.

Somehow the two sections got under way and reached Pewabic

Mountain in time for lunch amidst considerable hamming and speechmaking. The trip apparently was enjoyed. The mayor from a town near Boston, in drawing upon his stock of corn, called the tram the "Waltz Me Around Again" railroad. The trains reached Black Hawk about 6:00 P.M. and the excursionists arrived back in Denver several hours later.

One newspaper account had this to say: "All along the route of travel every aid was offered by the citizens, dynamite was exploded in thunderous welcome, and whistles tooted farewell." It can easily be imagined in what form the aid was made available. All expenses for the trip had been borne by the Central City Chamber of Commerce.

In reporting the event the *Denver Republican* headlined its story, "Oldest Mining District Shows That It Has Escaped Dangers of Mossbackism."

Even before the convention trip, excursions over the tram were infrequent. After discussing the matter of tram excursions with people who have firsthand information, it is safe to conclude that the tourist venture was not particularly successful.

In later years the solitary observation car was retained only for

No. 4 with festive garb for Democrat excursion in 1908. *Otto Blake.*

C.&S. superintendent Sol Morris on 1907 inspection trip. *Louis Pircher.*

the use of visiting officials and their friends. In the picture, Sol Morris and his party are about to leave the yard in Black Hawk for a tour of the line in 1907. Mr. Morris was the Colorado and Southern superintendent in Denver and later went to Chicago as a Burlington official.

The tourist angle was certainly worth a try. One lady said the ride over the tram wasn't any dirtier than a trip on the narrowgauge in the summer. There was one big difference, she claimed. It was harder to keep from falling out of the tram cars!

There was big time competition in the railroad tourist business. Gilpin County as seen from the tram didn't have a Royal Gorge, a Pikes Peak, or a Georgetown Loop. The tram fared better hauling ore.

End of the Line

Mine production in Gilpin County began to slump in 1914 and continued to drop through and following the war years. The Gilpin Railroad was doomed. Actually, mining had started to decline in 1906, the year the Colorado and Southern took over the line. The rosy picture of a profitable feeder line was shadowed by doubt and misgivings. The earnings dropped in direct ratio to the fall in mine production. It was not a question of why but when. This tells the story:

Year	Mine* Production	Freight** Earnings	Surplus**	Remarks
1904	$ 1,707,257			The Gilpin Tramway Co.
1905	1,764,283			" " " "
1906	1,435,842			The Gilpin Railroad Co.
				Gilpin Railroad
1907	1,283,855			" "
1912	1,330,796			" "
1913	1,035,746	$ 45,644	$10,238	" "
1914	770,655	17,603	—9,750	" "
1915	739,104	12,951	—10,437	" "
1916	709,603			International Trust Co.
				Trustee
1917	723,146			Suspended Jan. 17, 1917
1918	576,536			Sold June 2, 1917

* *Mining in Colorado*, C. W. Henderson, 1926.
***Poor's Manual of Railroads*. Neither The Gilpin Tramway Company nor Gilpin Railroad listed prior to 1914.

The Gilpin Railroad was doomed unless steps of some kind were taken to save it. The tonnage from the few operating mines was easily handled by several remaining mills. By January, 1917, the Polar Star was the only custom mill treating the county ores. Trucks were beginning to make inroads in the hauling business.

When the Gilpin Railroad was in its last throes, the Gilpin County branch of the Metal Mining Association heard a speaker say the county had been credited with a donation of $1000 for the benefit of good roads.

Service on the Gilpin Railroad was discontinued January 17, 1917. A paragraph in the Central City paper said, "There is nothing definite at the present time but reports indicate that the main line has been abandoned." The article went on to say that some ore is being hauled to the switch below the New York mill and loaded in cars at that point and hauled to the Iron City mill for treatment.

The *Idaho Springs Siftings News,* observing affairs in the next county, said on February 2, 1917: "A deal was consummated when W. L. Bush, president of the First National Bank, sold the entire issue of $67,000 worth of Gilpin Tramway Co. bonds to the Radetsky brothers of the Colorado Iron and Metal Co. It is the intention of the purchasers after foreclosing on the property and securing proper title to junk a portion of the tramway and its equipment and continue the operation of the biggest portion if it can be made to pay.

"Taxes have aggregated $3600 yearly together with $4000 annual interest on the bonds made it an unprofitable one for the C.& S. With a considerable reduction in taxes and slightly higher charges for hauling ore it is calculated that the tram could be kept in operation."

The Black Hawk council met on February 6, 1917. Mr. Fred N. Rogers appeared in behalf of the stockholders and read a petition asking for tax relief for the line for 1916. A report of the meeting said "council did not see fit to grant the petition," thus giving one of the few remaining industries of the town a further kick. Black Hawk councils through the years seem to move in the same direction.

By March 30, 1917, reports were in circulation to the effect that the Gilpin Railroad had reverted back to the stockholders. Radetsky was asking for the return of the deposit made with the offer. In any event the "deal" did not appear to be "consummated."

Further insight into the demise of the Gilpin Railroad can be obtained by study of Poor's *Manual of Railroads* for the years 1914, 1915, 1916, and 1917.

		Deductions	
Earnings freight	$45,638	Taxes	$1,652
other	6	Rentals	1,000
	————	Int on bonds	4,020
Total	$45,644		
Operating expenses		Total deduc.	$6,672
M of W, structure;	$ 6,721		
M of equipment	5,843		
Trans. expense	16,281		
Gen. expense	449		
	————		
Total	$29,294		
Net earnings	$16,350		
Other income	560		
	————		
Gross income	16,910		
Surplus for year	$10,238		
Total Surplus June 30, '13	40,741		

Funded debt outstanding June 30, 1913 consisted of $71,000
1st Mtge 6% of Gilpin Tramway Company due 1919

Officers A. D. Parker, Pres (VP C&S)
B. F. James, Sec't & Treas (same on C&S)
J. H. Bradley, General Auditor (same on C&S)

		Deductions	
Earnings freight $17,603		Taxes	$1,999
Operating expenses		Rentals	1,000
M of W and structures	$ 5,883	Int on bonds	4,020
Maint of equipment	4,893		————
Trans. expense	9,692	Total	$7,019
General expense	451		
	————		
Total	$20,919		
Deficiency from operations	$ 3,316		
Misc income	586		
	————		
Net deficit	$ 2,731		
Deficit for year	$ 9,750 (sic)		
Surplus forwarded	$40,741		
Surplus June 30, 1914	30,991		

Officers: Same as previous year

Earnings freight	$12,951
Operating expenses	
M of W and structures	$ 3,995
Maint of equipment	3,082
Transportation expenses	6,385
General	464
	$13,926
Deficit from operations	$ 994
Tax accruals	4,778
Total operating deficit	$5,754
Non-operating income	335
Balance deficit	$ 5,417
Charges	
Rentals	$ 1,000
Interest funded debt	4,020
Total charges	$ 5,020
Deficit for year	$10,437

Officers: Same as previous year

Funded debt outstanding $71,000 Gilpin Tramway Company First Mortgage 6% gold bonds dated May 15, 1899, due May 15, 1919 interest May 15 and Nov. 15 at Denver, Colo. Coupon bonds $500 each registered as to principal. Callable since 1909 on any interest date. Authorized $75,000 of which $4000 held in treasury.

Trustees International Trust Co.

Income tax: Interest payable without deduction of U.S. normal income tax.

Officers: Same as previous year.

This company ceased operations during the early part of 1917 and all property sold under foreclosure proceedings June 2, 1917.

Notes and records on file at the Colorado and Southern auditor's office in Denver tell a terse story:

Originally, June 24, 1906, acquired property of The Gilpin Tramway Company constructed to serve the mining industry near Black Hawk.

Capital stock $10 per share
Authorized   20,000 shares
Issued   20,000 shares
All of which is owned by the C.&S. Ry. Co.
Funded debt 6% bonds of The Gilpin Tramway Co.
Date mortgage   May 15, 1899
Maturity   May 15, 1919
International Trust Co., Denver, Trustee
Authorized issue $75,000
Outstanding   67,000

Operation of this property became unsuccessful and a decree was signed April 24, 1917, ordering the sale of the property and was entered in the district court, and property sold June 2, 1917, to A. H. Radetsky who dismantled the line and disposed of the salvage.

The C.&S. charged off in 1917 $63,306.69 as the cost of the stock owned.

Otto Blake, who some thirty years before had ridden engine No. 1 on the first trip over the line, was foreman on the salvage operation. Mr. Blake, now and for many years a gas and oil dealer in Black Hawk, operated a livery and contracting business in the town.

The Banta Hill line had been pulled up earlier. Blake completed the main salvage job in three months. There was a crew of six men besides Blake and the engineer and fireman, George Hughes and Amos Kerns. The track and appurtances were in such bad shape that dismantling was easy. Every piece of iron was taken to Denver and sold for scrap, as was most of the rolling stock with the exception of 20 cars which were retained with a piece of track between the New York and Iron City mills. The three engines were stored in a Denver junk yard until 1938 when they too went the way of all scrap iron.

The obituary notice, and perhaps the last news story of any kind about the Gilpin Railroad, or The Gilpin Railroad Company, or The Gilpin Tramway Company—sometimes known as the Gilpin Tram or the tram—appeared in the *Central City Register-Call* June 8, 1917:

M. S. and A. H. Radetsky of Denver bought at sheriff's sale at the court house the property of The Gilpin Tramway Co. Price was $60,000 represented by bonds of the company, which purchasers procured at 33c on the dollar.

All rails, spikes, engines, cars and other machinery were shipped to Denver and sold for what it will buy. The owners are in line for making a good sum of money on their investment.

Old grade between Frontenac and Russell.

Acknowledgment

Blake, Mary
Blake, Otto
Bloch, Don
Boulder Camera
Clerk and Recorder's staff, Gilpin County
Colorado and Southern Railway Company, The
Colorado's Little Kingdom, Donald C. Kemp
Crittenden, H. I.
Denver Post
Denver Public Library   Western History Department
Denver Republican
Denver Times
Engineering News
Fritz, Luella
Harrison, Paul R.
History of Colorado, Frank Hall
Laird, R. L., editor and publisher, *Weekly Register-Call*
Lind, Peter A.
Lundberg, George E.
Mining in Colorado, C. W. Henderson
Pierce, William
Pircher, Louis
Poor, M. C.
Poor's Manual of Railroads
Railroad & Locomotive Historical Society Bulletin No. 57
Rainey, D. A.
Rizzari, Francis
Robbins, Charles
Robbins, James
Rocky Mountain News
State Historical Society of Colorado
Trains
Weekly Register-Call
Westcott, Linn H.
Williams, George
Ziege, William